YOUNG PROFILES

Paul Joseph
ABDO Publishing Company

visit us at
www.abdopub.com

Published by ABDO Publishing Company 4940 Viking Drive, Edina, Minnesota 55435.
Copyright © 2000 by Abdo Consulting Group, Inc. International copyrights reserved in
all countries. No part of this book may be reproduced in any form without written
permission from the publisher.

Printed in the United States.

Photo credits: AP/Wide World; Shooting Star

Contributing editors: Tamara L. Britton, Kate A. Furlong

Library of Congress Cataloging-in-Publication Data

Joseph, Paul, 1970-
        'N Sync / Paul Joseph.
           p. cm. -- (Young profiles)
        Includes index.
        ISBN 1-57765-430-7 (hardcover)
        ISBN 1-57765-432-3 (paperback)
        1. 'N Sync (Musical group--Juvenile literature. 2. Rock musicians--United
States--Biography--Juvenile literature. [1. 'N Sync (Musical group)
        2. Singers] I. Title. II. Series.

        ML3930.N3 J67 2000
        782.42164'092'2--dc21
        [B]   00-034247

Contents

'N Sync

'N Sync is the music industry's **reigning** pop group. With their record-breaking **album**, *No Strings Attached*, 'N Sync has become more popular than the five members ever dreamed.

Lance Bass, JC Chasez, Joey Fatone, Chris Kirkpatrick, and Justin Timberlake make up the super group known as 'N Sync. 'N Sync burst onto the music scene in 1997, just a little over a year after they formed.

Within two years, 'N Sync had taken over the music industry with their clean, mellow harmonies and toe tapping grooves. People from Europe, Asia, Australia, South America, Canada, and of course the United States rush out to buy their albums and see them **perform** live.

'N Sync can be seen and heard everywhere. If you turn on the television you are sure to catch one of their videos. They have **performed** on countless award shows and talk shows. On the radio, 'N Sync can be heard on everything from pop stations to adult contemporary stations.

But success did not come overnight for these five guys. 'N Sync worked hard to develop their skills. They stuck together through the good times and the bad. And most important they never gave up on their dreams. 'N Sync's rise to fame began where dreams do come true—Orlando, Florida.

'N Sync performing in Orlando, Florida.

Profile of 'N Sync

The members of 'N Sync: (clockwise from the top) Joey Fatone, Lance Bass, Chris Kirkpatrick, JC Chasez, Justin Timberlake.

Joey

Full Name: Joseph Anthony Fatone, Jr.

Birth Date: January 28, 1977

Place of Birth: Brooklyn, New York

Home: Orlando, Florida

Family: Mother, Phyllis; father, Joe
Sr.; sister, Janine; brother, Steven

Favorite Food: Italian

Favorite Colors: Purple and red

Favorite Actor: Robert De Niro

Favorite Music: Musicals and
Movie Soundtracks

Favorite TV Show: *Friends*

Favorite Movie: *Goodfellas*

Favorite 'N Sync Song: "I Want You
Back"

Lance

Full Name: James Lansten Bass
Birth Date: May 4, 1979
Place of Birth: Clinton, Mississippi

Home: Orlando, Florida
Family: Mother, Diane; father, Jim;
    sister, Stacy
Favorite Food: French toast
Favorite Colors: Red and blue
Favorite Actors: Tom Hanks, Meg Ryan
Favorite Music: Brian McKnight, Garth
    Brooks
Favorite TV Shows: *Friends, I Love Lucy*
Favorite Movie: *Armageddon*
Favorite 'N Sync Song: "God Must Have
    Spent a Little More Time on You"

Chris

Full Name: Christopher Alan Kirkpatrick

Birth Date: October 17, 1971

Place of Birth: Clarion, Pennsylvania

Home: Orlando, Florida

Family: Mother, Beverly; sisters, Molly, Kate, Emily, and Taylor

Favorite Food: Tacos

Favorite Color: Silver

Favorite Actors: Adam Sandler, Jackie Chan

Favorite Music: Busta Rhymes, Beastie Boys

Favorite TV Shows: *The Simpsons, South Park*

Favorite Movie: *Big Daddy*

Favorite 'N Sync Song: "Giddy Up"

JC

Full Name: Joshua Scott Chasez

Birth Date: August 8, 1976

Place of Birth: Washington, D.C.

Home: Orlando, Florida

Family: Mother, Karen; father, Roy; sister, Heather; brother, Tyler

Favorite Food: Chinese

Favorite Color: Blue

Favorite Actor: Harrison Ford

Favorite Music: Brian McKnight, Seal, Sting

Favorite TV Shows: *Friends*

Favorite Movies: All the *Star Wars* and *Indiana Jones* movies

Favorite 'N Sync Song: "Bye, Bye, Bye"

Justin

Full Name: Justin Randall Timberlake

Birth Date: January 31, 1981

Place of Birth: Memphis, Tennessee

Home: Orlando, Florida

Family: Mother, Lynn; father, Randy; brothers, Jonathan and Steven

Favorite Food: Pasta

Favorite Color: Blue

Favorite Actor: Kevin Spacey

Favorite Music: Hip-hop

Favorite TV Show: *Seinfeld*

Favorite Movies: *The Usual Suspects* and *Twelve Monkeys*

Favorite 'N Sync Song: "God Must Have Spent a Little More Time on You"

'N the Beginning

There are many, many Boy Bands on the charts today. But one stands out from the crowd and that is 'N Sync. 'N Sync stands out because they put the band together themselves and were not prepackaged by **promoters** and **producers**. They also were very talented with each having distinct voices and moves.

'N Sync was formed through hard work and a little luck. Chris Kirkpatrick was living in Orlando and working at Universal Studios as a singer. It was there that he met and became good friends with Joey Fatone. Two other buddies, JC Chasez and Justin Timberlake were also working together in Orlando on the show *The Mickey Mouse Club*.

While doing *The Mickey Mouse Club*, JC and Justin were part of a talented group. Other Mouseketeers included teen pop stars Britney Spears and Christina Aguilera and *Felicity*'s Keri Russell. More importantly there were two other guys on *The Mickey Mouse Club* who were high school friends of Joey.

Chris had always wanted to put a singing group together. He thought that JC and Justin would fit perfect with he and Joey. All four had super voices and all four loved pop music. But the foursome was missing one key voice that would round out the group.

Justin called his vocal coach in his hometown of Memphis. The coach recommended the perfect guy, Lance Bass. Lance took a chance and jumped on the next flight to Orlando to meet four strangers. Little did they know that Lance was the final piece of what would end up being the hottest group in the world!

'N Sync in 1996.

Naming the Band

Besides working on their singing and **performing** the five guys needed a catchy name for their band. They thought about it for weeks but nothing seemed to fit these guys or their unique sound. Then one day Justin's mom was watching the guys practice and remarked how "in sync" their voices and dancing were. She then thought how about "In Sync" for the name of the band.

The guys didn't know about the name. The name of the band is something that would be with them forever. Justin's mom continued to work on the name. She started looking at the initials of their names. Then she looked at the last letter of everyone's first name and she came up with JustiN, ChriS, JoeY, LansteN, and JC. 'N Sync was born!

These five guys were completely 'N Sync. The name perfectly summed up everything about the band. Five guys with five diverse backgrounds, from five different parts of the United States, with different musical influences, somehow managed to come together and be 'N Sync.

Each member of the band brings his personal taste to the mix. Joey loves fifties and sixties groups like Frankie Lymon and the Temptations. Lance is into the country twang of Garth Brooks. Chris patterns his high voice after Michael Jackson. JC's vocal style is influenced by one of his favorite singers, Sting. And Justin throws in a little bit of Stevie Wonder's soul with hip-hop energy.

Justin's mother came up with the name 'N Sync.

Purely Original

Many singing groups today are put together by **producers**. 'N Sync, however, put themselves together before anyone else got involved. Justin thinks that has helped a lot, "We put the group together ourselves. I think that's something that's paid off in the long run because we were friends before we got a **management** team."

Lance agrees, "Everything that we do is always together, and I think that's what makes the group unique."

Shortly after forming as a group in 1995, the five guys worked hard to get noticed. They practiced singing and dancing together for many hours each day. 'N Sync didn't have a manager so they did all of the work themselves. They made a video and a tape of their music and sent it off to managers and record companies. 'N Sync also printed posters, picked outfits, and did their own **choreography.** They played anywhere they could get a job.

In 1996, about a year after 'N Sync formed, their hard work began to pay off. Lou Pearlman heard them play and offered to become their manager. Pearlman was the manager behind such super groups as New Kids on the Block and the Backstreet Boys.

'N Sync was very excited to have such a great manager but Pearlman was even more excited with 'N Sync. Pearlman sensed something different from other groups he had worked with. He believed they were purely original with their own certain style. Pearlman believed that before long these five guys would be the biggest band in the world.

'N Sync performing at halftime of the Orlando Magic game.

Taking Over Europe

Pearlman got 'N Sync a record **contract** at BMG in Germany. That meant that the five guys had to go over to Europe. But it didn't matter where they went. They just wanted to sing, make records, and **perform**.

The group packed up and went to Germany to make a record. They recorded their first single, "I Want You Back," and it was a smash. Within a few months of going to Europe, 'N Sync had a **gold record** on its hand. They even broke long-standing European records for the fastest selling single.

Their next song, "Tearin' Up My Heart," raced to number one as well. When 'N Sync's album was finally released it soared to number one within a week! Suddenly 'N Sync were pursued by frenzied fans wherever they went.

After releasing the album, 'N Sync began a concert **tour**. They started in Europe and then went to Mexico, South Africa, and Asia. Almost every show was sold out. 'N Sync couldn't go anywhere without being mobbed by fans. Anywhere that is but their home—the United States.

'N Sync was popular in Europe before making it big in the United States.

Heading Home

'N Sync was the hottest group everywhere in the world but the United States. In any country in Europe they couldn't walk down the streets without **body guards**. But in their hometown of Orlando all five could go to movies, walk down their streets, and lead normal lives. But that wouldn't last long either.

In 1998, 'N Sync returned to the United States to concentrate on making it big there. They loved their fans across the world but they knew if they wanted to really make it they would have to make it in the United States.

When their **album**, *'N Sync*, hit the stores in the United States everything changed. Within four months of releasing their album in the U.S. it went to the top of the charts.

Numerous television appearances followed. They filmed a Disney concert special, **performed** at the Miss Teen USA

Pageant, and made guest appearances on *The Tonight Show, Live With Regis and Kathie Lee,* and MTV.

They began their first U.S. concert tour and sold out every show. Life was now crazy for these five guys. They couldn't even walk outside their house because fans were camped there. Everything they worked so hard to accomplish was becoming reality. But that was only the start.

Thousands of fans line up everyday to catch a glimpse of 'N Sync.

A Crazy Schedule

For the next year 'N Sync was everywhere. They had a crazy schedule and typically only about five hours of sleep a night! They were either on an airplane or traveling on their bus across the United States. It wasn't easy being 'N Sync but the five guys wouldn't have traded it for anything.

'N Sync was constantly on the go. They would go from city to city living in hotels across the country. Their day usually consisted of rehearsing, meeting with record executives and their managers, doing an autograph session, and then ending the evening with a concert.

And then to top it off, 'N Sync was working on a new album. So they had to record for many hours a day. They rarely saw their family and when they did it was for short periods of time.

They were the hottest band in the entire world and 'N Sync couldn't have been happier. But then something happened that almost tore the band apart.

Despite their crazy schedule, 'N Sync was having a lot of fun.

Staying 'N Sync

In 1999, 'N Sync was involved in a nasty **lawsuit** with their manager Lou Pearlman. It almost broke up the band. When 'N Sync first formed they signed a **contract** with Pearlman that gave him 65 percent of all the money made by the band. That left the five band members with only seven percent of the profits per person! And the contract also stated that Pearlman owned the name 'N Sync and all of the songs.

The five guys were working 18-hour days nearly seven days a week. They believed that the contract was unfair and they wanted out of it. So in September of 1999, 'N Sync announced they were leaving Pearlman and RCA Records. 'N Sync was going to get a new **management** team that would treat them fairly and decided to sign a record deal with Jive.

Two weeks later, Pearlman and RCA filed a $150 million lawsuit against 'N Sync. The lawsuit claimed that a contract was signed and could not be broken for five years. Pearlman also said that if they fired him that they could not use the name 'N Sync.

The five guys were very upset. All they ever wanted to do was make music and **perform**. The lawsuit was taking up all of 'N Sync's time.

The lawsuit was settled later that year and 'N Sync won! They were all very happy. They could continue to use their name and signed a deal with Jive Records. In the end it all worked out for 'N Sync. In 2000, they put out one of the best selling albums in the history of the music business.

'N Sync continued to work and perform while they were involved in a lawsuit.

No Strings Attached

The **lawsuit** delayed the release of their new **album**, *No Strings Attached*. But when it came out people rushed out to buy it. 'N Sync was back and their new album took the world by storm.

No Strings Attached sold over a million copies the very first day! Never before in the history of the music business has that been done. Their first single, "Bye, Bye, Bye" hit number one in less than a week. 'N Sync was again the hottest band around.

In 2000, 'N Sync continued their hectic schedule. They toured the world, made videos, appeared on television and award shows, and signed thousands of autographs. When it was all over 'N Sync had played in five countries, hundreds of different cities, had traveled thousands of miles, and played in front of nearly a million of their fans!

Through the ups and downs, 'N Sync stuck together and never gave up. They believe the reason everything worked out is because they have the greatest fans in the world.

When 'N Sync released their album in 2000, it sold over a million copies the very first day.

'N Sync on the Web

www.nsync.com

Check out one of the best sites on the internet. 'N Sync's official site has the latest news on the hottest band. Also included are bios, photos, music, videos, and tour information. There is also an 'N Sync store to buy tickets to concerts and other fun merchandise. Sign up to receive emails from the band themselves!

Opposite page: (from left to right) JC Chasez, Joey Fatone, Chris Kirkpatrick, Justin Timberlake, and Lance Bass.

Glossary

Album: recorded songs put on a tape or disk to be sold and listened to.

Body Guards: people who protect entertainers from harm.

Choreography: putting together dance routines.

Contract: a signed agreement by two parties that says what each party is responsible for and must do throughout the length of the agreement.

Gold Record: selling a million albums.

Lawsuit: taking someone to court to try to recover something (usually money) that is believed to be theirs.

Manager: a person who represents a band or singer. The manager is responsible for getting record contracts, concerts, getting paid, etc.

Perform: to present entertainment to an audience.

Producers: people who are in charge of a play, television show, movie, or album.

Promoters: people who handle the advertising, publicity, or public relations for a band.

Reigning: to be at the top.

Tour: a set of dates where a band goes to many different cities and performs concerts.

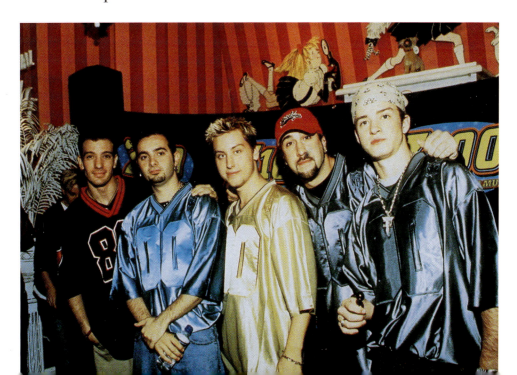

Index